THE KETO DESSERTS COOKBOOK

Sweet weight loss, tasty low-carb, high-fat dessert recipes.

2019 Edition

OLIVIA BRYAN

Table of contents:

Text Copyright 4

Legal and Disclaimer...4

Introduction..5

Gluten-free Chocolate Coconut Cupcakes..6

White Chocolate and Raspberry Keto Cake 8

Keto Lava Cake..10

Keto flourless chocolate cake 11

Sugar-free Caramel Sauce Recipe 13

Keto Protein Chocolate Chip Cookies...14

Chocolate Mint Cupcakes with Frosting 16

Keto Coconut Macaroons..17

No-Bake Coconut Cookies...19

Keto Sugar Cookies 20

Keto Pots De Creme 22

Paleo Keto Shortbread Cookies 23

Key lime pudding..25

Keto Vanilla Pound Cake...26

Keto Chocolate Mousse 28

Chocolate Peanut Butter Pecan Bark 29

Keto No Bake Cookies...31

No-Bake Keto Peanut Butter Chocolate 32

Avocado Popsicles..33

Strawberry Ice Cream...35

Lemon zucchini loaf..36

Low Carb Lemon Blueberry Donuts 38

Keto Lime Curd 40

No-Bake Keto Pumpkin Pie 41

Magical Frozen Fudge Pops..43

Cold-Brew Mocha-Coffee Panna Cotta...44

Low Carb Chocolate 46

Homemade Thin Mints..48

Keto Oreo Cookies..50

No Bake Low Carb Lemon Straw 52

Easy Orange Cake Balls 53

Almond Joy Chia Seed Pudding..54

Keto Coconut Mocha Donuts..55

Paleo Vegan Coconut Cranberry Crack Bars 56

Super Fudgy Paleo & Keto Brownies..57

Dark Chocolate Raspberry Fudge Tart..59

No-Bake Keto Chocolate Peppermint Cookie Bars..61

Keto Lemon Bars..62

Text Copyright

Legal and Disclaimer

Introduction

Are you interested in Keto? Is keto for you? Are you a good candidate for the Ketogenic diet? Why choose the Keto lifestyle? Exactly! Keto is a lifestyle choice, rather than a diet, and it is a lifestyle choice, which can offer a multitude of benefits. The keto alimentary program proposes the concept that your carbohydrate intake should be scaled down and controlled. One of the worst characteristics of dieting for most people is the hunger you feel as soon as you reduce the amount of food that you consume. However, some studies submit that low-carb consumption may actually reduce one's appetite. Wow! Lose weight without hunger pangs. That's a huge plus if you want to lose weight.

Keto Dessert Recipes are simply delicious. Interestingly, it allows the Keto dieters to eat some tasty and toothsome things while losing weight and staying in ketosis. The following recipes are tested and proven diets which you can maximise to stay healthy while trying to lose weight or look more attractive and agile:

Gluten-free Chocolate Coconut Cupcakes

Gluten-free Chocolate Coconut Cupcakes are grain-free cupcakes. They are packed with cinnamon, high-quality fats and chocolate. Cinnamon proves very helpful in stabilizing blood. The chocolate is rich in polyphenols. Go for Gluten-free Chocolate Coconut cupcakes when you are keen on ending the dinner on an extremely exciting note or when you want a mid-afternoon energy boost.

Makes: 20 cupcakes

Nutrition Information:

Calories 183/ Total fat 21.6g/ Total Carb 5.7g/Sugar 1.4 g

Ingredients: Cupcakes:

- 1 cup coconut flour, sifted
- 1/3 cup coconut cream
- 1/2 cup cocoa butter.
- 1/2 cup cocoa powder
- 1 tsp. apple cider vinegar.
- 2 tsp. vanilla powder
- 2 tsp. cinnamon.
- 1 cup of xylitol of sweetener of choice
- 1/2 tsp. baking soda.
- 250g grass-fed ghee or butter
- Pinch of salt

Icing:

- 1/4 cup cacao butter.
- 1/4 cocoa powder
- Pinch of salt.
- 2-3 tbsp. brain Octane Oil
- Xylitol or sweetener of choice
- 7 large eggs or 8 small-medium sized eggs

Garnish: Fresh berries

Directions:

- Heat the oven to 350' F(170'C).
- Add the butter and cacao powder to a small saucepan and heat to a medium heat. Apply all ingredients to the food processor and blend until they are smooth and creamy.
- Have a taste of the mixture and make amends if the need be.
- You can add a little sweetener of your choice or salt to improve the chocolate flavor.
- Scoop the mix into the pre-prepared muffin trays on an even proportion.
- Put them in the oven and bake for roughly 20 minutes.
- As the cupcakes bake, put the icing ingredients to a little saucepan and melt to a medium heat until wholly mixed.
- Have a taste of the icing mixture and enhance the sweetness if needed.
- Pour the icing mixture into a bowl and then place in the fridge to set.
- Remove the muffins from the oven and let them cool when they are thoroughly cooked and golden brown.
- Take out the chilled icing from the fridge and spread over the tops of the cooled muffins and embellish with berries.
- On the last note, store in the fridge.

White Chocolate and Raspberry Keto Cake

This keto white chocolate and raspberry cake is appealing and invitingly delicious. It is typically served with rich and creamy white chocolate sauce. Naturally, this flour darkens as it cooks. This creates a rich brown color in your keto cake without any added cocoa powder.

Nutrition Information:

Calories: 323/Total Fat: 31.5g/ Net Carbs: 6.6g/ Total Sugars: 4.8g

Ingredients:

Cake:

- 2 ounces of grass-fed ghee
- 5 ounces of cacao butter
- 1 cup green banana flour
- 1/2 cup of coconut cream
- 1/2 cup of granulated sweetener like Lakanto MonkFruit
- 2 teaspoons of vanilla powder or 3 teaspoons pure vanilla extract
- 4 eggs
- 2 teaspoons of apple cider vinegar
- 1 teaspoon of baking powder
- 2 cups of raspberries

White chocolate sauce:

- Pinch of salt
- 1/2 cup of coconut cream
- 2 teaspoons of pure vanilla extract
- 1/2 ounces of cacao butter

Directions for Cake:

- Pre-heat the oven to 280 degrees F.
- Mix all the dry ingredients until they are completely combined.
- Set the raspberries aside and add the remaining ingredients and mix until they are thoroughly mixed.
- Line a loaf tin or a 8-inch cake with baking paper and pour in the cake mix.
- While scattering the raspberries over the cake mix, reserve some for garnishing.
- Place in your oven and bake for about an hour or until strong.
- Prepare the sauce while it bake

Directions for Sauce

- Mix all the ingredients in a saucepan on low heat
- Take the mixed ingredients out of the cool and harden
- Put the sauce on the pieces of cake when serving
- Scatter extra raspberries on the cake and serve

Keto Lava Cake

Keto lava Cake is a low-carb dessert made with cocoa powder rather than a wheat flour. It is a keto approved sweetener. Keto lava cake is creamy, moist and tasty. This recipe does not require any sort of low carb flours. It is probably one of the best keto desserts. You can make this perfect keto desserts with only 5 ingredients. For a more enjoyable time, you can serve it with low-crab ice-cream. Keto lava cake dessert only has a total of 8g of carbs but only 4g NET carbs.

Cook Time: 12 Mins/ **Prep Time:** 5 Mins/ **Total Time:** 17 Mins

Nutrition Information:

Calories: 192/ Fat: 15g/ Carbohydrates: 8g

Ingredients:

- 4 tbsp cocoa powder
- 2 eggs
- 3 tbsp heavy whipping cream
- 1 tbsp vanilla extract
- 1/2 tsp baking powder
- 3 tbsp sweetener erythritol

Directions:

- Preheat your oven to 350 degrees F
- Mix your cocoa powder, erythritol and whisk
- Beat your egg until it is fluffy in a different bowl
- At this point, add your heavy cream, vanilla extract and egg to the erythritol and cocoa mixture
- Sprinkle a little cooking oil into the mug, add your batter and put it to bake for roughly 15 minutes at 350 degrees F

Keto flourless chocolate cake

Keto flourless chocolate cake is a flourless chocolate cake essentially for low carb keto dieters. As a very simple dessert, it only requires five basic ingredients. It will interest you to know that it is a simple cake that doesn't take too much efforts, ingredients and time to make.

Prep Time :15 minutes/ **Cook Time:** 45 minutes/ **Total Time:** 1 hour

Servings 12

Nutrition Information:

Calories 295kcal

Ingredients

- 1/4 teaspoon salt
- 1/3 cup water
- 12 ounces unsweetened baking chocolate
- 4 large eggs
- Boiling water
- 1/2 cup low carb sweetener
- 2/3 cup butter or ghee which is cut into tablespoon size pieces

Directions:

▢ Line the beneath of 9-inch spring-form pan with parchment paper.

▢ Heat water and salt in a small pot and heat to a medium heat until sweetener and salt dissolve.

▢ You can melt baking chocolate in a microwave or double boiler.

▢ One at a time, put in egg and beat well after adding each.

▢ Put the mixture into a pre-prepared spring-form pan. Position spring-form pan in a bigger cake pan and put boiling water to the pan outside which should be 1 inch deep.

▢ For 45 minutes 350' F, bake cake in water bath.

Sugar-free Caramel Sauce Recipe

Caramel sauce recipe is low in carb and sugar-free offering the keto dieters delicious meals to lose weight and burn their fats. This recipe only requires four ingredients and 10 minutes to be fully cooked and prepared. This is so easy and simple to make.

Cook Time: 10 minutes

Nutrition Information:

Calories 91 kcal/ Fat 9g/ Total Carbs 0g/ Net Carbs 0g

Ingredients

- 1 tsp Vanilla extract
- 2/3 cup Heavy cream
- 3 tbsp Sukrin Gold
- 2/3 cup Butter (salted)

Directions:

▢ Melt the Sukrin Gold and butter together in a medium-large saucepan over low heat.

▢ When it has melted, go ahead and cook for about 3-4 more minutes

▢ Stir it from time to time until golden brown.

▢ Ensure it keep a watchful eye on it to avoid burning

▢ Add the cream and reduce heat to a gentle simmer. Simmer should last for 7-10 minutes,

▢ Stir occasionally until the mixture takes on a caramel color. At this level, it must be thick enough to coat the back of a spoon.

▢ Get the stuff out of the heat and whisk in the vanilla extract.

Keto Protein Chocolate Chip Cookies

Chocolate chip cookies help in balancing your blood sugar and giving you enduring energy. These Chocolate Chip Cookies provide nutrient-dense fats and gut-healing collagen protein. To have a delicious afternoon snack, dip the chocolate chip cookies in your bulletproof. Chocolate Chip Cookies offer a satisfying dessert.

Prep Time: 15 min./ **Total Time:** 45 min.

Makes: 16 delicious cookies

Nutrition Information:

Calories: 128/Total Fat: 11g/ Total Carbs: 4.7g/ Sugar Alcohols: 67g

Ingredients:

- 3 tbsp. grass-fed Bulletproof Ghee
- Butter
- 2 cups blanched organic almond or hazelnut meal
- Birch tree-sourced xylitol or stevia
- 3 tbsp. Bulletproof Collagen Protein
- 1 tsp. apple cider vinegar
- Baking powder
- A pinch of salt
- 1 tsp. apple cider vinegar
- 1/3 cup high quality, sugar-free chocolate, chopped

Directions:

- Pre-heat the oven to 170°C/340°F.

- Lubricate and line two baking trays with parchment paper.

- Pour the collagen protein, salt, baking powder and the almond meal into a bowl.

- Add the apple cider vinegar to the baking powder. Give it some minutes to react.

- Pour the remaining ingredients to the bowl and stir until it is evenly combined

- Have a taste of the dough and make amends if the need be

- At this point, roll the mix into balls and place them on the lined baking tray.

- Keep the ball full if you want chewier and softer treats.

- Press the balls flat if you want crunchier cookies. Use your hands to shape them.

- Put the cookies in the oven and bake for roughly 15 minutes or until golden brown.

- Get them out of the oven when they are fully done.

- You can put the cookies on a wire cooling rack.

Chocolate Mint Cupcakes with Frosting

Serving Size: 1 cupcake with 1 tbsp of frosting

Nutrition Information:

Calories: 265/ Fat: 21g/ Carbs: 7g net

Ingredients:

For the Cupcakes:

- 1/2 cup coconut butter/manna
- 1/4 cup, plus 1 tablespoon coconut flour
- 1 tbsp ground flax seeds
- 1/2 cup coconut butter/manna
- 1 tsp vanilla extract
- Pinch of salt
- 1/4 cup Swerve, or other granulated sweetener
- 1/2 cup coconut butter/manna
- 1 tsp vanilla extract
- 1 tsp baking powder
- pinch1 tsp vanilla extract

For the Frosting:

- 2 tbsp swerve or another granulated sweetener
- 1/2 tsp matcha powder
- 1 tsp vanilla extract
- 1/2 cup full fat coconut milk
- 1 cup raw cashews

Directions:

- Preheat oven to 350F.
- Lubricate and line 6 wells of a muffin tin.
- Add water to coconut butter and stir until it is smoothly combined
- Mix the salt, vanilla, swerve and flax. Allow these settles for a few minutes for the flax seed to get all.
- Mix baking powder and coconut flour in a separate bowl.
- In a gradual manner, put in flour mixture.
- Stir until everything is even such that there are no lumps.
- Create a division into muffin tins and bake for 20-25 mins
- This baking should go on until the tops are strong and the edges are turning golden. Remove them from the oven and wait a few hours for them to cool

Keto Coconut Macaroons

Keto coconut macaroons are low-crab and flourless coconut macaroons. They are chewy, flavorful and soft. Keto Coconut Macaroons are fortified with collagen protein. In a matter of 15 minutes, they are fully cooked. Interestingly, these keto macaroons recipe makes 9 large cookies. However, you can make it smaller if you like. Just watch the cook time If you make them smaller. It will be closer to 10 minutes when they're lightly browned and done.

Serves: 9

Nutrition Information:

Calories: 105/Fat: 7g /Carbs: 10g (includes 8g carbs from sugar alcohol)/ Sugar: 1g

Ingredients:

- 5 tablespoons birch xylitol
- 1 scoop Vanilla Collagen Protein Powder
- 2 pastured egg whites
- 1/2 teaspoon pure almond extract
- 1/2 teaspoon baking powder (aluminum-free)
- 1 1/2 cups unsweetened shredded coconut

Directions:

- Preheat oven to 325 degrees F.

- Place all dry ingredients in bowl and stir until is mixed evenly mix.

- Add egg whites and almond extract and stir well to combine.

- Scoop 9 equal servings and put them on a parchment-lined or silicone baking mat lined or baking sheet.

- Bake for about 15 minutes or until macaroons are lightly browned.

- Use a spatula to remove the macaroons from baking sheet and allow to cool before eating.

No-Bake Coconut Cookies

No-bake coconut cookies are dairy-free, low-carb and gluten-free.

Prep Time: 5 minutes /**Resting Time:** 5 minutes/ **Total Time:** 5 minutes

Servings: 8

Nutrition Information:

Fat: 34.2g/ Carbohydrates: 6.8g/ Sugar: 3.1g

Ingredients:

- 3/8 cup organic coconut oil
- 1/2 cup xylitol
- 3/8 tsp salt
- 3 cups organic unsweetened shredded coconut

Directions:

- Pour the all ingredients in a blender or a food processor

- Mix together until they are well blended such that they stick together

- Take away the mixture from the food processor/ blender

- Decorate with cocoa or carob powder and shredded coconuts

- Leave for some minutes to become firm.

Keto Sugar Cookies

These keto sugar cookies are sweet and light. They offer a perfect treat for holidays and cookie cravings. They really look fancy with a dip in silky coconut icing. You can mix your keto sugar cookies with a hot cup of Bulletproof Coffee or a turmeric latte. You can also add them to your holiday cookie plate with Christmas classics like Mexican wedding cakes.

Nutritional Information (Per Cookie):

Calories: 168/ Total Fat: 15.9g/ Total Carbs: 5.2g/Sugars: 0.5g

Sugar cookie ingredients:

- 3 tablespoons coconut flour
- 1 egg
- 3 tablespoons coconut oil or grass-fed ghee
- 1 teaspoon baking powder
- 1 cup blanched almond flour
- 2 teaspoons powder or vanilla extract
- Pinch of salt
- 1 tablespoon granulated sweetener
- Pinch of salt
- 2-3 tablespoons granulated sweetener liquid stevia or Lakanto

Icing ingredients (optional):

- 1 teaspoon raw cacao (optional)
- 1 tablespoon granulated sweetener
- 2 tablespoon coconut cream
- 4 tablespoons grass-fed ghee or coconut oil

Directions:

- ☐ Preheat the oven to 356 degrees F.

- ☐ Mix the ingredients in a bowl or blender until it becomes a dough that holds together when pinched.

- ☐ Spread out the parchment paper and place the dough on top.

- ☐ Spread another sheet of parchment on top and carefully roll.

- ☐ Cut sugar cookies into shapes by using a small glass or cookie cutter.

- ☐ Put parchment sheet into a baking tray and place in the oven.

- ☐ You can bake for 15-20 minutes or until slightly golden.

- ☐ Cookies will look soft and will harden when it is cool.

- ☐ Place them in the fridge for 10-15 minutes before dipping in icing.

Keto Pots De Creme

Total time: 15 minutes

Serves: 2-4

Nutritional Information (Per Serving):

Calories: 267/Total Fat: 24g/ Total Carbs: 16g. /Net Carbs: 4.7g /Sugars: 1g.

Ingredients:

- small pinch of salt
- 1/4 cup hazelnuts
- 5 tablespoons cocoa powder
- 1 teaspoon liquid stevia
- 3 large avocados, skin and pits
- 2.5 ounces 100% dark chocolate
- whipped coconut cream
- Raw nuts

Directions:

- Combine all ingredients in a food processor

- You can now process pot de creme base until it is smooth such that no chunks of avocado remain.

- Put the chocolate paste into ramekins or small bowls.

- Put in the fridge for a minimum of 2 hours to thicken up

Paleo Keto Shortbread Cookies

These are light and buttery keto shortbread cookies. These cookies require only a few ingredients and little bake time including low-carb ingredients that won't give you a cookie crash. Grass-fed butter is the major ingredient when trying to create a buttery consistency in these keto shortbread cookies. Grass-fed collagen peptides puts a protein boost without changing the flavor. This recipe includes a chocolate glaze and also serves as a very good base for any flavor variation.

Nutritional Information (Per Cookie):

Calories: 375/Total Fat: 29.5g /Total Carbs: 17.6g/ Net Carbs: 7.9g / Sugars: 3.3g

Shortbread ingredients:

- 1/2 teaspoon vanilla extract
- 1 tablespoon (8g) coconut flour
- 1/4 teaspoon fine sea salt
- 1/3 cup (145g) almond flour
- 1/4 teaspoon fine sea salt
- 1/3 cup plus 1teaspoon grass-fed butter
- 1 vanilla shortbread collagen protein bar

Directions

☐ Mix all shortbread ingredients until they are combined in a food processor. Leave out collagen in the mix.

☐ Remove the mix from the food processor and lay out the dough rolling pin until it is about 3.5mm thick.

☐ Reduce the cookies to curly round cutter and freeze for 30 minutes.

☐ Preheat oven to 350 degrees F.

☐ Line a perforated baking tray with a silicone liner or parchment.

☐ Get cookies out of the freezer, place on the baking sheet, and bake for roughly 8 minutes or until golden.

Key lime pudding

Prep Time: 5 minutes /**Cook Time:** 5 minutes/ **Total Time:** 1 hour 10 minutes

Nutritional Information:

Calories 171/ Fat 18g/ Carbohydrates 1.7g

Ingredients:

For Pudding Ingredients:

- 3 Tbsp Melted Coconut Oil
- 1-2 Tsp Almond extract or Vanilla
- 2/3 cup Erythritol Simple Syrup
- 1.6 oz Lime Juice
- 2 ripe Avocados or 200 mg
- Pinch of salt
- 2/3 cup Erythritol Simple Syrup

For Erythritol Simple Syrup Ingredients:

- 1/8 -1/4 tsp Xanthan Gum powder
- 6 drops of liquid Stevia
- 1 tsp vanilla extract or maple
- 1 cup boiling water
- 3/4 cup erythritol

Directions:

- Make a small heavy bottomed pot available

- Add stevia, erythritol, the water and the extract to the pot.

- Turn to low medium heat.

- Stir from time to time until it boils.

- Allow the syrup decrease and become firm for roughly 3-5 minutes.

- Switch off the heat and splash the Xanthum gum over the water.

- It will thicken up when you whisk it.

Keto Vanilla Pound Cake

Keto Vanilla Pound Cake is an awesomely simple dessert with perfect macros. Keto Vanilla Pound cake has the right amount of sweetness. The pound cake also stores very well in case when there are left-overs!

Prep Time: 15 minutes / **Cook Time**: 50 minutes / **Total Time**: 1 hour 5 minutes

Nutrition Information Serving Size: 1 Piece (65 grams or 1/12 of cakes):

Calories: 249/ Fat: 20.67g /NET Carbs 5.23g

Ingredients

- 4 large eggs
- 2 ounces cream cheese
- 1/2 cup butter
- 1 cup erythritol
- 2 cups almond flour
- 1 tsp vanilla extract
- 2 tsp baking powder
- 1 cup sour cream

Directions:

- Preheat oven to 350 degrees Fahrenheit.

- Luxuriously butter a 9 inch bundt pan.

- In a large bowl, mix almond flour and baking powder.

- In a separate bowl, cut butter into curly round cutter, adding cream cheese.

- Microwave cream cheese and butter for 30 seconds. More importantly, don't burn cream cheese.

- Mix the wet ingredients together until completely combined.

- Add vanilla extract, erythritol and sour cream to cream cheese and butter mixture. Stir well.

- In a big bowl full of baking powder and flour, pour the wet ingredients. Stir well.

- Apply eggs to batter and stir them well.

- At this point, put batter into buttered bundt pan and arrange in oven.

- Bake for a period of 50 minutes or until a toothpick position in the cake emerges spic and span.

- For two hours, let cake cool wholly. The cake may crumble a bit if you remove them it too soon.

Keto Chocolate Mousse

Keto Chocolate Mousse is a low carb dessert which serves as a fat bomb and suits the macros for a fast fat recipe. Interestingly, Mousse is nearly zero crab.

Servings: 4

Nutrition Information Per Serving:

calories 227 / 24g Fat/ 1.5 net carbs

Ingredients:

- 2 oz cream cheese
- 3 oz heavy whipping cream, whipped
- 2 oz unsalted butter
- 1 tbsp cocoa powder
- 2 oz cream cheese
- Stevia, to taste

Directions:

- Soften butter and add it with sweetener
- Stir it until it is completely blended
- Put cream cheese and blend until it is smooth
- Put in cocoa powder and blend totally
- Use spoon to put the mixture into small glasses and refrigerate for 30 minutes.

Chocolate Peanut Butter Pecan Bark

A Chocolate Peanut Butter Pecan Bark is a carb-free chocolate treat. It is made with healthy ingredients. It is a best fit for late-night sweet tooth. Interestingly enough, this recipe is dairy free and gluten free. Chocolate Peanut Peacan Bark can easily be made without the nuts.

Prep Time :15 minutes/ **Cook Time** :45 minutes/ **Total Time** :1 hour

Servings: 25

Nutrition Information Per Serving:

Calories: 85 / Fat: 10g/ Carb: 1g/ Sugar: 5 g makes 25 piece

Ingredients:

- 1/4 Unsweetened Cocao Powder
- 1 Cup Coconut Oil
- 1 Tsp Vanilla Extract
- 1/4 Cup Creamy Peanut Butter with no sugar added
- 1/4 Cup Unsweetened Cocao Powder
- 1 Tsp Almond Extract
- 1/4 Tsp Sea Sat
- 1/2 Cup Creamy Peanut Butter (no sugar added)
- 1/2 Cup Swerve (or stevia)
- 1/2 Cups Unsweetened Shredded Coconut

Directions:

☐ Start by whipping heavy whipping cream until it exhibits stiff peaks in a medium mixing bowl

☐ Add peanut butter, cream cheese vanilla, and stevia in a separate bowl.

☐ Mix them on medium speed until they are smooth.

☐ It is ideal to keep it in the refrigerator overnight and served the next day.

Keto No Bake Cookies

Keto No Bake Cookies are fudgey, crunchy and creamy. These are three key words to describe these awesome keto no bake cookies. These amazing cookies offer you a juicy way to satisfy your cookies cravings and sweet tooth. More importantly, you can derive important macronutrients from keto no bake cookies.

Nutrition Information:

Calories :174/ Carbs 6 g./ Sugar 1.2 g.

Ingredients:

- 2 Tablespoons real butter
- 2/3 cup all natural peanut butter or nut butter
- 1 cup unsweetened natural shredded coconut
- 4 drops of vanilla stevia or sweetener

Directions:

- Melt the butter in a microwave safe dish.
- Stir the peanut butter together until it is smooth.
- Add coconut and stevia and mix well.
- Spread a sheet pan and scoop spoonfuls on them.
- Freeze for 5-10 minutes.
- Store them in a sealed bag.

No-Bake Keto Peanut Butter Chocolate

This keto dessert has low sugar, low carb and high fat. All these make the recipe a perfectly delicious keto dessert or fat bomb. This peanut butter chocolate is gluten-free.

Nutrition Information:

Fat: 23g/ Carbohydrate: 7g/ Sugar: 1g

Ingredients:

For the bars:

- 2 oz butter
- 1/2 cup peanut butter
- Vanilla 1/2 tsp
- 1/4 cup swerve icing sugar style
- 3/4 cup almond flour

For the Topping:

1/2 sugar free chocolate chips

Directions:

☐ Stir all the ingredients for the bars together and spread them into a small 6 inch pan.

☐ You can melt the chocolate chips in a microwave for a period of thirty minutes.

☐ Lay out the topping on the top of the bars.

☐ Put the bars in the fridge for a minimum of 1 hour until the bars thicken up.

Avocado Popsicles

Avocado Popsicles are ideal keto recipes for the summer period.

Prep time:30 minutes/**Total time:**30 minutes

Ingredients:

- 2 Tbsp of Lemon Juice
- 6 Tbsp Sugar Alternative
- I Cup of unsweetened almond milk
- 2 Medium Avocados
- 2 Tbsp of Lemon Juice

Chocolate ganache:

- 10g (2 tsp) of Cacao Butter
- 80g of Low Carb Chocolate

Directions:

- Pour the two avocados, sugar alternative and lemon juice into the mixer

- Mix properly and occupy all of the molds with the mixture

- Place it into the freezer to freeze.

- Take one frozen ice pops and dip them into the cooled chocolate.

- You can eat it right away or put it back into the freezer.

Strawberry Ice Cream

Strawberry is low carb, gluten Free and dairy free

Ingredients:

- 16 oz frozen strawberries
- 1/2-3/4 cup equivalent sweetener
- 2 cans (13.5 oz) coconut milk
- 16 oz frozen strawberries
- 1/2-3/4 cup equivalent sweetener

Directions:

- Mix all the ingredients in a blender and blend until they are smooth.

- Put the mix into your ice cream maker

- Process it in accordance with manufacturer's directions.

- Put the strawberries on the ice cream.

- Put the ice cream in the freezer for 1-2 hours to become firm.

Lemon zucchini loaf

Servings: 18

Nutritional Information:

Calories: 143/ Total Fat: 13g/ Total Carbohydrates: 2g/ Net Carbohydrates: >1g

Ingredients:

For the Loaf:

- 2 teaspoons baking powder
- 1/2 teaspoon xanthan gum
- 1/4 teaspoon salt
- 3 large eggs
- 1 teaspoon vanilla extract
- 1 tablespoon lemon zest
- 2 tablespoons fresh lemon juice
- 1 cup zucchini shredded
- 1/2 cup coconut oil, melted

For the Glaze:

- 4 tablespoons lemon juice
- 1/3 cup Swerve confectioners

Directions

- Heat to 325 degrees F

- Ensure you line a loaf pan with parchment paper.

- Combine baking powder, salt, the flour and xanthan gum.

- Whisk together eggs, vanilla, lemon juice, oil, sugar and Swerve granular in a separate bowl

- At this point, fold in the dry ingredients with the wet.

- Fold the lemon zest and zucchini into the batter.

- Transfer to the loaf pan and bake for about 50 minutes.

- You can mix together lemon juice and Swerve confectioners and lemon juice.

- Add loaf with glaze.

Low Carb Lemon Blueberry Donuts

Nutritional Information:

Calories: 109 kcal/ Total fat: 10.22g. /Carbohydrate: 6.32g

Ingredients:

- 1/2 cup coconut flour
- Sweetener equivalent to 1/2 cup sugar
- 2 tsp baking powder
- 2 tsp lemon zest
- 1/4 tsp salt
- 4 large eggs
- 1/4 cup avocado oil
- 1/4 cup freshly squeezed lemon juice
- 1/4 cup water.
- 1/2 tsp vanilla extract
- 1/2 tsp lemon extract.
- 1/2 cup fresh blueberries

Directions:

- ☐ Ensure you preheat the oven to 325F

- ☐ Lubricate the donut pan thoroughly

- ☐ Mix the baking powder, sweetener, coconut flour, lemon zest, and salt together in a big bowl

- ☐ At this point, stir in the oil, lemon juice, eggs, oil, lemon juice, water and extracts until they are thoroughly mixed

- ☐ Calmly fold in the blueberries.

- ☐ Add the donut cavities about 3/4 full with batter and bake 18 to 22 minutes until they become firm to touch.

Keto Lime Curd

Nutritional Information:

Calories: 34

Ingredients:

- 1/2 Tsp Salt
- 4 Tsp Coconut Oil
- 1/3 cup Erythritol
- Stevia
- 4 large eggs

Directions:

▢ Put the egg yolks inside a heavy bottomed small pot.

▢ Turn the heat up to medium and begin to stir.

▢ Stir over and over again and add stevia after two minutes

▢ As you stir it gradually, add the erythritol

▢ Be careful not let the mixture boil as you stir the Lime Curd for 3-5 minutes.

▢ The next step is to add the coconut oil and keep stirring until the mixture starts to bubble.

▢ Note that the curd will harden when it becomes cold

No-Bake Keto Pumpkin Pie

Serves: 6-8

Nutritional Information (Per Serving):

Calories: 199/ Total Fat: 17.2g/ Total Carbs: 11g./Net Carbs: 5.7g/ Sugars: 4.5g.

Ingredients:

- 3 cups desiccated coconut
- 2 tablespoons coconut cream
- 1/2 to 1 tablespoon sweetener like non-GMO erythritol or birch xylitol
- 1 tablespoon melted grass-fed ghee or coconut oil

Pumpkin filling ingredients:

- Pinch of salt
- 1/4 water
- 2 teaspoons vanilla extract
- 2 teaspoons Collagelatin
- 3 tablespoons coconut oil, ghee or butter
- 1/2 cup coconut cream
- 2 teaspoons Ceylon cinnamon
- 1/4 cup water
- 15 ounces steamed pumpkin

Directions:

⬜ Add desiccated coconuts and blitz until they become very fine in a food processor.

⬜ Put the remaining crust ingredients to your blender and combine again until they become thoroughly mixed.

⬜ Lubricate and Line a 9-inch cake pan or pie plate with parchment,

⬜ Suppress the mixture with your hands

⬜ Get it packed down as soon as possible with the back of your spoon.

⬜ Refrigerate to set.

⬜ Serve cold with keto vanilla ice cream or whipped coconut cream.

Magical Frozen Fudge Pops

Prep Time: 10 min.

Servings: 4 pops

Nutritional Information:

Calories 303 /Total fat 26g/ Total Carb 6g/ Sugars 2g

Ingredients:

- A pinch of salt
- 1 tsp. vanilla powder
- 2 pasture-raised egg yolks
- Monk fruit sweetencr to taste or liquid stevia
- 2 tbsp. Collage Latin
- 1/2-1 tbsp. unsweetened chocolate powder
- 2 tbsp. Brain Octane Oil
- 1 tbsp. cacao butter
- 1 tsp. vanilla powder
- 270 ml (1 cup) coconut cream

Directions

☐ Combine the Collage Latin, chocolate powder, cacao butter, brain octane oil, salt, chocolate powder and salt

☐ Heat on low.

☐ Remove from the heat once the mix has simmered and all the ingredients have melted and combined together

☐ Allow to cool until room temperature.

☐ Add egg yolks, liquid mix and sweetener when it has cooled

☐ Pour into ice-block molds and place in the freezer until set.

☐ You can drizzle melted cacao melts or dark chocolate on the top

☐ Optionally, you can also sprinkle with organic berries and edible flowers

Cold-Brew Mocha-Coffee Panna Cotta

Serves: 2

Nutrition Information (per serving):

Calories: 110/ Total Fat: 7g/ Total carbs: 11g/ Net Carbs: 5.25g/Total Sugars: 0g

Ingredients:

- 1 Tbsp filtered water
- 1 ¾ tsp grass-fed gelatin
- 1 11-ounce container of Mocha Cold-Brew Bulletproof Coffee
- Toasted coconut

Directions:

- Add the gelatin and water in a small saucepan

- Stir it to combine.

- Remove for a minute or two to allow it to come up and thicken.

- Add in ¼ cup of the cold brew mocha when the gelatin has bloomed

- Heat on low until the gelatin has absolutely dissolved.

- At this point, add the remaining cold brew and stir to combine.

- Spoon the mix into 2 small glass jars

- Refrigerate them to set taking about 1 to 2 hours.

- Serve and enjoy.

Low Carb Chocolate

Prep Time: 10 minutes/**Cook Time:**20 minutes

Servings: 13 servings

Nutrition Information:

Calories 170 kcal/ Total fat 16g / Total Carb 3.5g

Ingredients

- 140 grams (5oz) unsweetened baking chocolate chopped
- 30 grams (1oz) whey protein powder
- 3/4 teaspoon liquid stevia extract
- 70 grams (2.5oz) powdered erythritol
- 140 grams (5oz) cocoa butter

Directions:

◻ Blend protein and erythritol together into a superfine powder, resulting into a smoother chocolate.

◻ Set up a double boiler setup or a small saucepan over low heat.

◻ Put cocoa butter and heat it

◻ Stir it from time to time until it melts.

- Add baking chocolate and stirring repeatedly until smooth.

- Remove from heat and continue to stir until very smooth.

- Put in the fridge to cool and consequently hardened.

- Store and enjoy at room temperature.

Homemade Thin Mints

Prep Time: 30 mins/ **Cook Time:** 30 mins/ **Total Time:** 1 hour

Nutrition Information:

Calories: 116 kcal/ Total Fat 10.41g/ Total Carbohydrates 6.99g

Ingredients:

For Cookies:

- 1/3 cup cocoa powder
- 1/4 tsp salt
- 1 large egg slighten beaten
- 1/2 tsp vanilla extra
- 3/4 cups almond flour
- 1/3 cup swerve sweetener

For Chocolate Coating:

- 1 tsp peppermint extract
- 1 tbsp coconut oil and butter
- 7oz lily's dark chocolate

Directions:

Cookies:

- Pre-heat the oven to 300 degrees F

- Ensure you grease and line two baking sheets with parchment paper

- Mix cocoa powder, almond flour, sweetener, baking powder and salt in a big bowl

- Put in butter, egg and vanilla extract

- Stir well until dough sticks together

- Bake cookies until firm for roughly 30 mins

Chocolate Coating:

- Put a metal bowl on a pot with slightly simmering water

- Put the cookies into the chocolate

- Use two forks to turn them over

- Refrigerate until fully set

Keto Oreo Cookies

Prep time: 20 minutes/**Cook time:** 15 minutes/**Total time:** 35 minutes

Servings: 24

Nutrition Information:

Calories: 86 kcal/

Ingredients:

- 1 egg
- 128 g erythritol
- 1/2 teaspoon xanthan gum
- 1/4 teaspoon espresso powder
- 1/2 teaspoon xanthan gum
- 1/2 teaspoon baking soda
- 3/4 teaspoon salt
- 144 g almond flour
- 13 g black cocoa powder
- 37 g cocoa powder

For Vanilla cream Filling:

- 4 g coconut oil
- 1 1/2 teaspoon vanilla extract
- Pinch kosher salt
- 56 g grass-fed butter
- 63-125 g Swerve confectioners

Directions:

- In a medium bowl, combine cocoa powder, xanthan gum, salt, baking soda and salt

- Whisk the mix until well combined

- Set aside.

- In a big bowl with an electric mixer, start to cream butter in a large bowl for 1-2 minutes

- Bring in sweetener and continue to beat until thoroughly mixed and add in egg

- At this point, wrap cookie dough with saran wrap and put in the fridge for 1 hour or overnight.

No Bake Low Carb Lemon Straw

Nutrition Information:

Calories: 474 kcals/ Fat: 48.2g / Net carbs: 5.3g

Ingredients

- 3/4 cup heavy whipping cream
- 1/3 cup Swerve sweetener
- 2 large strawberries
- 2 teaspoons lemon extract
- zest of 1 lemon
- 3 oz softened cream cheese

Directions:

- Combine the sweetener cream, cheese and whipping cream in the mixing bowl

- You can beat the mix until it is creamy and smooth

- Put in lemon extra and mix thoroughly

- At this point, chop one of the strawberries into little pieces

- Use half of the cream cheese mixture to fill each jar half way

- You can make a nice layer by adding chopped strawberry to both jars

- Put them in the fridge until ready to eat

Easy Orange Cake Balls

Prep Time:10 mins/**Cook Time:**10 mins/**Passive Time:**10 mins

Servings: 15 balls

Ingredients:

- Pinch of salt
- 1/3 cup coconut flour + more for rolling
- Zest of 2 navel oranges
- Heaping 2/3 cup almond butter
- 1/4 cup orange juice
- 35 drops Sweetleaf vanilla creme stevia to taste
- 1/2 tsp vanilla

Directions:

- In a mixing bowl, mix together all ingredients.
- Add a drizzle of avocado oil or a splash of orange juice.
- In the case where the mix is too wet, put in a sprinkle of coconut flour.
- Use small cookies to make balls.
- Squeeze them smooth and into your desired shape using the palms of your hands.
- Gently roll each ball in a bowl of coconut flour which should be about 1-2 Tbs.
- Let them cool for 10 minutes to thicken up

Almond Joy Chia Seed Pudding

Prep time: 10 mins/**Cook time:** 1 hour/**Total time:** 1 hour 19 mins

Servings: 4

Ingredients

- 2 cups unsweetened almond milk or coconut milk
- 1/2 cup unsweetened coconut flakes divided
- 1/4 cup unsweetened cocoa powder
- 1/4 cup powdered erythritol
- 1 tsp pure vanilla extract
- 1/3 cup chia seeds
- 2 tbsp crushed roasted almonds
- 1/4 cup sugar-free dark chocolate chips optional

Directions:

- Mix all the ingredients in a large bowl

- Beat cup chia seeds until smooth and even

- Bake for roughly I hour

Keto Coconut Mocha Donuts

Nutrition Information:

Calories: 161/ Total Fat: 14g/Carbohydrates: 2/Sugars: 1g

Ingredients:

- 1/2 tsp baking powder
- 4 eggs
- 1/2 tsp baking soda
- 1/4 cup coconut oil
- 1 Tbsp liquid stevia
- 1/3 cup unsweetened almond milk
- 1/2 tsp instant coffee granules
- 3 Tbsp unsweetened cocoa powder
- 1/3 cup coconut flour

Directions:

- Pre-heat the oven to 350
- Pour all ingredients into a mixing bowl and mix thoroughly.
- Add the mixture to a doughnut pan
- Bake for roughly 20 minutes
- Allow to cool and serve and enjoy

Paleo Vegan Coconut Cranberry Crack Bars

Ingredients:

- 1 cup coconut oil, melted
- 1/2 cup unsweetened cranberries
- 1/4 cup sticky sweetener of choice
- 2 1/2 cups shredded unsweetened coconut flakes

Directions:

☐ Add your cranberries, coconut and pulse in a food processor or high-speed blender

☐ Mix until they are well combined.

☐ In a mixing bowl, add your coconut oil, cranberry mixture and sticky sweetener of choice.

☐ Mix until fully combined.

☐ Gently lubricate your hands and then press firmly into the place.

☐ Refrigerate until firm.

Super Fudgy Paleo & Keto Brownies

Prep Time: 15 mins/**Cook Time:** 20 mins /**Total Time:**35 mins

Nutrition Information:

Calories: 102 Kcal

Servings: 16

Ingredients:

- 70g almond flour
- 2 eggs
- 1/2 teaspoon salt
- 80g cocoa powder
- 140-200g xylitol
- 130g unsalted grass-fed butter

Directions:

- Pre-heat to 350 degree F.

- Grease and line the buttoms and sides of a 8x8 inch baking pan with parchment paper.

- Add sweetener, cocoa powder, butter and salt to a medium heatproof bowl.

- Add one egg and whisk it well before putting another one.

- You can then add the almond flour and whisk strongly until completely blended.

- Bake for 15-25 mins.

- Allow to cool on a rack

Dark Chocolate Raspberry Fudge Tart

Prep time: 10 mins/**Cook time:** 35 mins/**Total Time:** 45 mins

Ingredients

- 3 eggs
- ½ cup coconut oil
- ¾ cup Swerve Sweetener
- 1 tbs vanilla extract
- 1 cup almond flour
- ½ cup low-fat cocoa powder
- 1 tsp baking powder
- a touch of salt
- 1/3 cup sugar-free dark chocolate chips.
- 1 ½ cup frozen raspberries
- 1 tbs water
- 2 tbs Swerve Sweetener

Directions:

- Pour the frozen raspberries into a pan and ensure you heat it with water

- In a large bowl, combine thoroughly eggs, sweetener, coconut oil and vanilla extract.

- Mix the cocoa powder, almond flour, sat and baking powder in a separate bowl

- Add the dry Ingredients to the water while stirring

- Remove the tart from the oven when it is done

- Let it cool and decorate and serve.

No-Bake Keto Chocolate Peppermint Cookie Bars

Start to Finish: 1 hour (15 minutes active)

Serves: 10

Nutritional Information (Per cookie bar):

Calories: 123/ Total Fat: 11g/ Total Carbs: 7.3g /Net Carbs: 1.5g/ Total Sugars: 1.5g

Ingredients Cookie Bars:

- 3 cups shredded coconut.
- 2 tablespoons MitoSweet
- 2 tablespoons grass-fed ghee.
- 6 tablespoons collagen protein
- 4-6 drops food grade peppermint essential oil.
- 3 teaspoons vanilla extract
- Pinch of salt

Ingredients Chocolate Drizzle:

- 2 tablespoons cacao powder.
- 3 tablespoons ghee
- 1 teaspoon vanilla extract
- 1 tablespoon MitoSweet

Directions:

⬜ Add coconut and blend on medium to high speed until evenly chopped in a blender .

⬜ Apply the remaining cookie bar ingredients and blend until thoroughly mixed. Leave out the collagen.

⬜ Line a loaf pan with parchment.

⬜ Scoop out the ingredients into the tin.

⬜ Use a spoon to evenly press down the mixture and then freeze until they are strong enough to slice.

⬜ Carefully remove bars from the pan and slice.

Keto Lemon Bars

Prep Time: 15 min/**Cook Time:** 45 min/**Total Time:** 1 hour

Yield: 8 servings

Nutrition Information:

Calories: 272/ Fat: 26g/Carbohydrates: 4g net

Ingredients:

- 1/2 cup butter
- 1 3/4 cups almond flour
- 1 cup powdered erythritol.
- 3 medium lemons
- 3 large eggs

Directions:

- Combine 1 cup almond flour, butter, 1/4 cup erythritol, and a pinch of salt in a big bowl

- Press the mix finely into an 8×8″ parchment paper-lined baking dish.

- Bake at 350 degrees F for 20 minues.

- Allow to cool for 10 minutes.

- Chop one of the lemons, juice all 3 lemons and add the eggs, 3/4 cup erythritol, 3/4 cup almond flour and pinch of salt into a big bowl.

- Mix evenly to make filling

- Having poured onto the crust, bake for 25 minutes.

- Serve with a sprinkle of erythritol and lemon slices

Printed in Great Britain
by Amazon

32552061R00036